My Journey From When We Were Colored

(Reality Writing)

My Journey From When We Were Colored

(Watered Down Through Integration)

Sallie Williams

To order additional copies of this book, contact:
Xlibris Corporation
1-888-795-4274
www.Xlibris.com
Orders@Xlibris.com
74782

CONTENTS

Dedication

I dedicate this book to my precious daughter Nicole who left me too soon, my grandson Sherrick an only child rejected by his own mother, and my two lovely sons, Norris and Chauncy all whom I love dearly.

INTRODUCTION

"Reality Writing"

Do you ever wonder what a person is thinking? What is on someone's mind when they seem to be in a far off place? Have you ever thought about something that you wanted to know but feared it might be taken the wrong way if you just asked? Let me take you into my zone, to share some of my thoughts with you. My motivation for writing this comes from a situation that has happened and it has triggered some of the things that I can remember from the past, things that I have observed through the years, and things that are happening now. In comparison, I am truly in awe of how much things have changed and not necessarily for the better and it has me "wondering", where did we go wrong. I have no scientific proof on the things that you will read, it is just what I think about, there is no research, and it is strictly from what I have analyzed. "I am a very deep thinker" and in my mind I look at things probably differently from others so as I take the journey from when we were colored, I am letting you hitch a ride with me, sharing my innermost thoughts with you.

My intent is not to offend anyone, merely point out things that have changed (as I see them), drastically, have been forgotten, "totally" ignored, or just phased out, from the way we dress, speak, how situations are handled, and things that is now permissible. I am merely just thinking aloud and I am sure everyone has something on his or her "mind" but some are afraid to reveal it to others. As I take this journey, some of the things that I "think" about, pretend it's an "imaginary rock" being thrown and if it hits you, well you'll know, don't get upset, just say "ouch". Now go and get your popcorn, kick back and take this journey with me and just maybe you will actually see what I "wonder" about.

MY JOURNEY FROM WHEN WE WERE COLORED

Watered down through integration

As I reminisce on how it was when we were colored, life "to me" was pleasant and simple. As a child, I never thought about the struggles my parent's experienced, explaining to the "rent man" that they would not have the rent until Friday nor did I think about how they were going to put food on the table because they never showed signs of despair. They never argued in front my two siblings, or me I am sure that they probably argued, but we never heard them. My dad was to me a "strong yet quiet easy going man that worked on "one" job for thirty seven years and only called in sick just one time and that was because he broke his foot "on the job". That was really a blessing in disguise because it happened during the hurricane season and "Carla" had "whirled" into town. If she had not, I just know that daddy would have tried to go to work had he not been injured. He could tell you down to the penny what his paycheck was going to be (that was amazing to me) and he stayed on that one job until he retired.

Now daddy and mama did not send us to church, they took us to church every Sunday and we would sing all the way there (in harmony) and all the way back home, actually we sang all of the time, (music was one of our gifts). Mama was the disciplinarian of the two, not harsh or "abusive" but she kept us in check. We never really got into any serious trouble unless you call going to bed pretending to be asleep without doing the dishes, of course that didn't work because mama would wake us up during the middle of the night to clean the kitchen, other than that she didn't have many problems out of us. My father was the provider always of the house and mama never had to work if she did not want to although she did help at the church kindergarten and she also played the piano at church, but that was her choice. Occasionally she would have my brother, sister and me sing together usually at church functions and I will have to admit we were good singers. It is too bad that opportunities were not readily available then as they are now, because I know without a doubt, we would have made it professionally.

Our recreation back then was very simple, daddy made my brother's kites with pages from the newspaper, glue, and from small limbs taken from a tree or pieces that he would stripped from and old plank, he did have to buy the string though. Sometimes he would use the Sunday's comic section to make it more colorful and that kite flew just as high as the ones that you would buy in the store or in my mind even higher. Guns back then were "play" toys and not the real thing and just about every boy or girl got a set (play guns) for Christmas. My sister was the lucky one because she also got the cowgirl outfit to go along with it and a bicycle also. I on the other hand got a big tricycle, I never made it up to the "big bike" but it did not matter, I was happy any way, and we never rode out of hearing range from mama. I can remember that my brother got a red wagon and he probably got a baseball glove and some other stuff, toys were not high tech with high prices as they are now.

Since the store bought gifts only came once or twice a year, we made our dolls with soda pop bottles, a clothes pen to wedge in a piece of rope for the hair and we'd just unravel the rope and we had a doll and dressed her up with old rags. My brother used to play marbles with his friends, I never knew the concept of the game I just would see them draw a circle in the dirt and try to knock the marbles out of the circle, I don't know if they kept score or not. Our horses were from old broomsticks and our hand was used as the switch hitting our own behinds to make the "horse" go faster. Some games we might have made up as we went along, some were not like "Little Sally Walker", "one two three red lights", hide and go seek, etc.

Back then the "village" really did raise a child because I can remember if my brother wandered to for from home, all mama had to do was go stand on the front porch and yell "John Jr.!!" (He really is a III). Mama would just go back into the house and you can rest assured that by "word of mouth" no matter how far he had sneaked off from home. My brother could have been a mile away and he was going to get that message, someone was going to tell him "your mama's looking for you" it was just like we had a Morse code or something. Now my sister and I were usually two or three houses down playing, pick up sticks, jacks, exchanging and reading comic books, (I sure wish I had known that they would become valuable, we would be rich now).

It did not matter what type of house that you lived in and 1 don't recall seeing trailer houses but if my friends did live in one, we were there to play and not to "poke fun". I probably would have thought that was cool house and would have wanted to live in one myself, people were not criticized for where they lived.

Our pets might have been a cricket or a grasshopper that we caught and placed in a jar poking holes in the top for air. We would take a piece of bacon and tie it to a string and go fishing in the "ditch" for crayfish; (we called them crawfish). A stray dog that was probably a mutt "dropped off' in the neighborhood was a prize pet. Do you know that dog would be fed the best food because my father (since buying dog food was expensive), would go to the neighborhood grocery store and ask the butcher if he had any scraps (parts they were going to throw away). If they did, daddy would take it and cook that meat, season it very well and have it smelling so good I wanted to taste it but it was for the dog. We once had a Collie and named it "of course" Lassie, he or she (I do not remember which was so attached to my brother that he or she would not let anyone harm him. I cannot remember if Lassie wandered into the neighborhood or if he or she was given to us but that is how things were back then.

I do not see grasshoppers anymore or the little doodle bugs (that is what we called them) that was the little bug that turned into a fragile little ball if you slightly touched it. I don't "hear" crickets anymore nor do I see "lighting" bugs or fireflies (they're the same) that use to light up the night, I no longer see the black caterpillars that turned into beautiful butterflies I haven't seen a lady bug either. They are all extinct where I live and "I think" that is because they sprayed pesticides to kill those annoying mosquitoes but "guess what", the mosquitoes are still here and everything else is gone.

When we got tired of playing, we would go home and "fix" a snack. That snack might be a syrup sandwich, a mayonnaise sandwich, I even made sugar and melted butter sandwiches, (we created our own). I use to make "meatless" hamburgers (everything on the bread accept the meat) I'd have to imagine that, "hmm" I wonder if that would be considered child neglect. I remember that it only took one fryer to feed our family of five (not a whole bucket) and we did not starve. Mama knew how to cut that chicken into so many pieces it was just as if we had the bucket and she fried it by using "lard" and no one in our family was obese. If we had cholesterol we did not know it and I am still here at age sixty five.

Casualties of War against the Mosquito

(Extinct in my Neighborhood)

| Grasshopper | Dragonfly | Beetle | Cricket |

| Praying mantis | Caterpillar | Butterfly | Ladybug |

Firefly

Man trying to kill the mosquito, caught these "Gods Creatures" in the crossfire, none survived. They had no protect ion (I wonder) who should do jail time as Mike did.

The Survivor/ the Victor

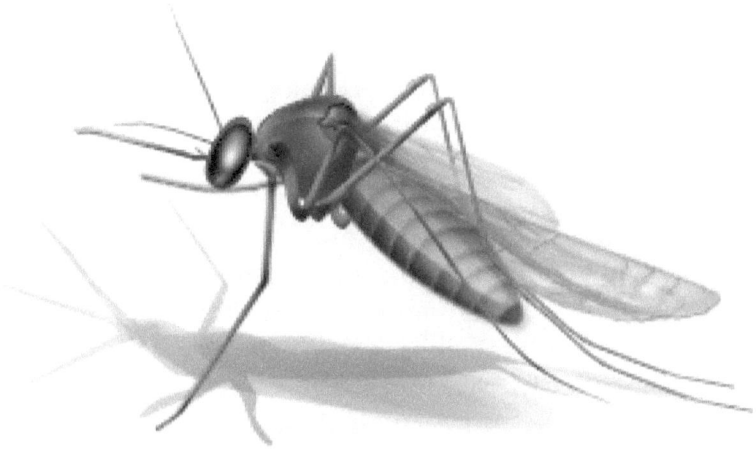

Every since the sixties, the city has sprayed chemicals to kill the mosquito and they keep coming back every year (go figure). Stagnant water "I guess" keeps them coming.

All of the food was in it's natural stage back then, chickens were grown naturally, not rapidly and was tasteful, peaches (that was my favorite) were large "furry" and "sweet" you could actually bite into to one and not worry about breaking a tooth and they were so juicy, the juice would trickle down your chin. Milk was "fresh" delivered to your doorstep; a "horse" pulled vegetable wagon would come through the neighborhood selling "fresh" fruits and vegetable. We lived in the city so it was exciting just to hear that horse clopping down the street and the vendor yelling "watermelon man" and one of us would run into the house to tell mama and daddy that he was outside just in case they did not hear him. Those watermelons were so big and guaranteed sweet, the vender would cut a plug in it for you to taste for yourself (he already knew that he had the sale) you could imagine the taste just from the smell along, your mouth would start to watering up, I really miss those things (my mouth does not water up any more). Occasionally we would ride to the farmers market to check out the produce, everything was fresh from the farm "not sprayed with chemicals" and if it was, you could still smell the freshness. Nowadays I can walk down the "vegetable and fruit" aisle in the stores and not smell a thing "I guess" the "preservatives" or whatever takes away the smell.

I remember, "walking" to the store on the corner if I had a quarter, and I would buy my favorites, a big sour pickle and a peppermint stick, a bag of potato chips (the bag was full back then), a bottle of soda pop which really had a "kick" back then they weren't flat like some are today, they even sold "green" plums back then I don't see those anymore, I wonder if they (plums) were a remedy for something. We knew when a candy bar was to old and had been on the shelves to long because it would have worms in it and had to be thrown away (someone was losing money). Nowadays you can eat last years candy, well I won't say its kept that long anymore, they do put an expiration date on everything now but expired items are still on the shelf being sold at a "reduced" price so you eat at your own risk. I still "wonder" though, where did the worms go? I often wonder what was put in the candy to keep the worms out and if it kills the worms, then what is it doing to us "hmmm"? I "remember" when a bag of flour and cornmeal had to be thrown away because there were "weevils" in them if it had sat on the shelf to long, not any more (someone was losing money) I wonder about that also, just what's keeping the weevils out, we're eating whatever made them extinct also.

Weevil

Whatever killed them, (I wonder) did it get us also? We are just bigger but I still (wonder) if we were caught in a crossfire also.

We did not have to go to the pharmacy to get something for "acid reflux" or "heart burns" all we needed was a "Coke or a Pepsi" and one good "burp" cleared that right on up (that does not work anymore). Go and look up the words "coke and pepsin" and you will see that it means an enzyme secreted in the stomach aiding in the digestion of proteins (someone saw a gold mine) it only cost a dime for a cure. Now we have digestive problems, heart failure, autism, kidney failure, diabetes; the list just goes on. Most of the "serious" complications that we knew of, only "old people" had, now all ages have the same problems. I wonder, why they say drink a coke or orange juice if your sugar drops to low then I imagine what happens to those that just drink it every day. Nowadays there is a dialysis center every five miles if not closer, and a pharmacy is even closer at least two or three in a one block radius. Just "imagine" how many pills there are all over the country and they all have side effects, you clear up one problem and encounter another, now "ask yourself" why does almost everyone have some type of medical problem? I "wonder" what is happening to us and, what is causing our bodies to break down and some at such a young age.

Now I am kind of ahead of myself on this journey but what I am about to tell you rather fits in here.

My boy's, (when they were infant's), baby formula which I prepared, (doctors orders) was a can of evaporated milk, an equal amount of "boiled" water, the clear syrup, and a couple of drops of baby vitamins and they never had problems. On the other hand, my daughter who is nine years younger than her brothers, formula (doctor's selection) was already sitting on the store shelves probably before she was born. She was diagnosed as a diabetic at the age of six, "hmm I wonder". Ya'll stay on this journey with me now and keep in mind, these are some of the things that "I think" about, it is not scientific facts. I wonder if there is a "class action" lawsuit floating out there somewhere and I just do not know whom to target. "Old" people" were the only funerals I can remember going to, (not any more).

When we were "coming down" with something (that is what it was called back then), we were kind of excited because that was our opportunity to get in the car and ride through the "neighborhoods" on our way to the drug store (miles a way). There was not one on every corner like there is now. We did not even concern ourselves with the fact we were going to have to take whatever medicine it was that mama bought, (castor oil, three sixes, cod liver oil, Scott's emulsion), the list of remedies was much longer, those are just names that I remember. Mama even had some "hog hoofs" in the medicine cabinet; I do not know what that was used for. I been told that people who lived in the country were given "cow chip tea" (now I could not believe that one) especially after they told me how it was made.

Anyway while we were out, we knew we were going to get an ice cream cone or something so we were happy for a brief moment, we weren't thinking about the fact that when we got home, we were going to have to line up and swallow some of that stuff from the drug store YUK! "But" we were very seldom ill. One time my brother sprained his ankle playing "street" football on the vacant lot across the street from our house, well daddy just got some "clay and some vinegar" and wrapped that ankle very tight, and let it heal by itself. That was not considered "child abuse" that was just an "old folk remedy", he probably would go to jail for that now. Let me go on record to say, I wouldn't suggest to anyone to try that because every thing nowadays has been "watered down" and doesn't have the same potency anymore and just keep in mind I'm only reminiscing.

Going to the doctor was almost unheard of then and we probably went just to get immunization shots. I recall that we had to sit in the back of the doctor's office on some wood planks in sort of little "screened in" porch that would seat six average sized people "crammed in like sardines" and just wait until all of the others up front who were sitting on "plush" furniture had been waited on. We did not complain, (well maybe to our selves we did) but that is the way it was then, take the bitter with the sweet. We finally got a chance to sit in the front after the "movement", that is how I found out the seats were plush.

REMEMBERING SAFER TIMES

There was a time when we could walk along the streets day or night and felt safe. We could go "trick or treating" and not have to check our "goodies" for razorblades being placed in apples, poison in our candy or whatever else that's malicious (I wonder how that got started). We didn't concern ourselves with, sex offenders, pedophiles, and never even thought about being abducted I'm not saying that I know for a fact that they didn't exist, they may have, I'm just comparing how it was then to how it is now and wondering why I wasn't afraid back then. I am now curious to know, "what changed"? I remember when I was a "child", Halloween was a day we as "children" looked forward to just to receive a lot of goodies, we couldn't afford to buy that much candy and that's what it was all about back then to a "child", now it's a "pagan" holiday and that means we shouldn't participate.

I can recall the orange city bus very well, and how we had to walk a mile and a half just to ride one. The bus did not come in our neighborhood (we knew to go straight to the back) but if you got lucky back then, you might catch a ride with someone that you might not even know, and "safely", arrive at your destination. I know some of you have heard this story before but you are riding with me on "my journey" and these are just things I often think about.

There is a middle school not as far from our old homestead closer than the bus stop was but I could not attend because I was "colored" and you know it makes me "wonder", how we lived so close to our neighbors. You could actually throw a "rock" into their backyard but there were not disturbances of any kind, they (our neighbors) did not bother us and we did not bother them.

I am aware that things have change and I know that we cannot live in the past but I do know how it was back then, I do not recall ever seeing police cars roaming our neighborhood at any time. If there were drugs around at the time, I knew nothing about it, I could have been too young to know but I am sure if there were drugs, they were probably filter into our area but were not given to children, I do not know. There was not a lot of violence then if there was, it never made it to the "the big newspapers" (I wonder why) and by chance that it did, it definitely was not "front page" news. We had our "own" colored newspaper and it circulated through out the "colored" communities. You know back then we were scattered all over the city, the areas that we live in mostly identified by wards or gardens, there were "first through six wards, Trinity garden "etc". We also had, and still have, an "Independent Heights" and my grandfather was the third and last "Mayor" before they were annex to they to the city (shout out). Violence was very rare back then because "the village" really did patrol our neighborhoods and children knew that there parents would find out about it if they misbehaved, there was no such thing as "not snitching", yep we (as kids) told on you if you did something wrong. If an adult told another parent that their child was acting up, there was no sense in trying to deny it, you couldn't just say that you didn't do it because your mama would just say to you, "I guess Mrs. Village is lying on you "huh" and you knew then, that wasn't going to work. We had not "intermingled" with other races back then so everything was controlled and patrolled by the parents and the village. What our parents called "thugs" and "fast girls" back then were like choirboys and girls (compared to kids today). They were thuggish amongst their peers and I guess they got that name because they probably got "caught" smoking a cigarette or drinking a beer, and or "overheard" cursing. Whatever they were doing back then, they would cease doing it if they saw any adult coming; they were respectable to all adults back then and even greeted them by saying how you doing ma'am or sir until the adult had passed by, then they would continue to do whatever it was that they were doing. There was not any high jacking, purse snatching, or car stealing, very few people had cars back then but I do not recall anyone's car stolen *when we were colored".

THE TRANSFORMATION

Then along came the transformation, we went from being colored and became black, that was a significant moment in my journey because we were no longer offended being called black by others. We were not so defensive about it, "thank you James for neutralizing the word and making it "proud" although we hadn't thought any less of ourselves, but the change "from colored to black" seem to have given us more confidence and power to embrace our "blackness". Others no longer offended us anymore that were around the same time that we were adjusting to another situation, integration (give or take a few years); now that changed how some of us felt about ourselves. The boldness we had gained, accepting who we are, started to dissipate; some of our "ethnic features" began to disappear. The "afro" became a joke, our "look" began to "change", our hair started getting longer and longer, it became so long that some had to "snap" their heads backwards just to keep it out of their faces. Eyes began changing colors they kept getting lighter and lighter (green, blue, hazel), our diction began to change (not that we were speaking improperly), we just did not sound the same anymore. It is like the "pride" was gone and now we were ashamed of our blackness. To "me" it was just like choosing the white doll over the black doll but this time, it was the "live" version, we felt the need to camouflage our looks. How can someone interview a child asking which doll he or she prefers while they are looking like the white doll themselves (my thoughts ya'll)?

Those of you that weren't around when we were colored probably don't even have a clue as to what I'm talking about because you were born "after" the metamorphosis started to take place and everything to you, would be "normal" but for me, it's like our "defining" features were starting to disappear just like the crickets did. Please understand, I did not say that there is something wrong with change, I am just merely "thinking" and it seems like a contradiction to me. The fact that one moment we were black and proud and the next, we were trying to cover up our features but of course this is "my journey" and you're just along for the ride, I am glad that I'm able to see all of the changes though.

I "think" our "ethnic" features are just a little bit to "dominant" for some to have hair down to the waistline and extremely light colored eyes, you know "black doll, white doll" and when I heard the question asked, does the baby have "good" hair, well, I did not see the humor. You no that has me wondering, if people in the "spotlight" are afraid of rejection, you know like not getting a certain part in a movie, not being an idol or the sit-com will be cancelled if all of their "own" characteristic traits are visible. You can wear what you want to, I am not knocking it, I am just wondering.

I wonder if anyone other than me notices these things or am I the only one. I wonder, are they told what hairstyle to wear or is it by chose, just curious. I don't see many of our hair styles anymore and I'm not talking about the "afro", I'm speaking of a style I might want my beautician try on me without having to buy bags of hair although I do have "cow licks' in the top so one bag might not be so bad. I would like to thank our "First Lady" Indie, Ericka, Tracie and even you to Condi and everyone else that keeps it real. To me, your beauty "shines" brightly "I said to me" simply because there are so few of you and it's speaks "volume" it's like you are saying, you are not afraid to embrace what God gave you and you don't give in to peer pressure. Let us keep in mind now that this is still "my journey" and I am letting you inside my mind sharing things normally that I would not say. (Can you see what I am thinking)?

I can remember when we started moving out of our old neighborhood, "there wasn't anything wrong with that move", after all I did tell you that we went "fishing" in "ditches". The only sad part about the move was, some of us no longer wanted to live by each other, and for those that thought they had "moved" up, well they hadn't, all that they had done was just moved over and formed another (?) community. There was even a change within families also. You remember me telling you about how my father made kites from "scratch", he also made walking stilts for us to play with, and how he stayed on one job (a steel company) for thirty-seven years and he could figure out what his paycheck was going to be down to the penny "hmmm"?

What I did not mention was the fact that he only had a six-grade education. He stopped going to school so that he could go to work to help his mother/my grandmother (a single woman) make ends meet. Daddy was our "plumber" if the commode was stopped up and the plunger did not work, he would go dig in the backyard, find the pipe and unstop it, he was our "mechanic" for minor car repairs, and there were many other things that he could do. To me he was one of the "smartest" men that I knew to say that he was born in 1911, I would say his education was equivalent to a high school graduate now (it didn't matter to me then or now how far that he went). Since we have all come together with "blended communities", it seems his education is an embarrassment to one of my family members in particular. It has been said as though they are ashamed of daddy's background. By the way they are in the group that thought that they had moved up, but they only had just moved over and the sad thing is the area where they moved to is so crime infested and it even made "national" news coverage, now what do you think about that? Just compare what daddy knew then to what he could do now if he had the same opportunities afforded to others nowadays. On mama's side of the family, there are educators and ministers so that's the only side spoken of very highly and in a positive manner, but thank God, mama was smart enough to choose daddy.

I remember a time when it was spoken," gray hair" meant a person with wisdom, someone respected, and a person to give sound good advice. Since times have changed, now it just means that you are an "old" senior citizen" and you should just get somewhere and "sit down" because you are in the way and you have nothing to offer. Now I was born with gray hair and I was told that it was a sign for good luck (I did not think so) and by the time I was forty, because of my "hair color" (I had not aged), I was getting senior citizens discount offers. I am eligible now but nobody wants advice now and respect is limited. I guess nowadays you have to "color" your hair so it will not cause too much attention. I "wonder" if people realize that unless they are "rich" and can "afford" a complete over haul, all of they are doing is just covering up the gray, everything else still looks the same. Don't get me wrong, there's absolutely nothing wrong with changing your hair color I'm thinking about changing mine, but I've observed that you don't see many "gray haired" women on television unless they are advertising "dentures, diapers, or wheelchairs", stay with me now, my thoughts only.

I wonder why society does not realize s that "seniors" still have capabilities and plenty to offer. Do people think that all seniors should be in the "pasture" grazing? I think I can still sing with some of the best, and there are others with talent but there is a "cut off" to participate unless you are already established. I "wonder" why there are not any reality shows with older people competing, the motor skills might be slower but they are still functioning. I wonder why the elderly aren't respected anymore; children use to listen but not anymore but If you just stop and think about it, an elderly person really is a "walking library" with knowledge dating back even before their time to the present. I am thinking there are many serious problems and they are out of control but now that I am a "senior village person", the rules have changed and we am not allowed to settle anything because now no one wants to hear what we have to say. I still drive a car and I drive the "speed limit" so that makes me the bad driver and since I am not speeding, I get yelled at or, get the "finger" I wonder why.

As you can see, I'm really not a "writer" and I don't claim to be, I'm saying what's on my mind so there is no chronological order like there was when I first started but this "my journey" and nowadays anything goes so just get some more "popcorn" and try to stay with me. Everything nowadays is a "reality" situation so just consider this, "reality writing".

DEEP THINKING

Now ya'll read this part very carefully, I don't want to be misconstrued because I'm not bashing, passing judgment, nor could I care less one way or the other on "most" of these issues (whatever floats your boat). These are just some of the things that I often "wonder" about and some of the things that "some" of you want to know too but you are afraid to ask. I wonder why do we have to bow to the queen, rise for the judge, and stand for the president? I wonder how the "king" of rock and roll was chosen. Who decides who are the ten most beautiful women in the "world" are and what was it based on, personality, wealth, or looks? Then I wonder if those women selected actually believe that. I often think about all the extremely "obese people and what caused that, we all seem to be obsessed with food "I think" something "addictive" must have been added but it affected everyone differently (my thoughts ya'll) and if I'm repeating myself, keep in mind that I'm not a "writer" okay? I wonder how many blacks were told back then that their two front teeth needed to be pulled and I wonder how many fell for that one. The reason that I think about that one is because I had seen several people of "color" with their two front bottom teeth missing and I remember that I was told that my two needed to be removed. I decided to wait until they start to give me trouble and guess what, those are "almost" the only two that I have left fifty years later (imagine that).

I "wonder" sometimes about "gays and lesbians"; did God actually create three genders? Were they actually born like that? Was there something the mother was taking (prescribed medicine maybe) during the pregnancy? Were there that many in the "closet" back then, is it one of the "side effects" caused by taking prescription drugs, or is it just a lifestyle? (I am just curious, not judgmental). I often "wonder" just whose getting "royalties" for all of the inventions and discoveries by black people. I know the real-estate tycoons and the hotel giants, children benefit from there parents wealth but I wonder what family member is benefiting from the stop lights and the peanut discoveries, are there any "heirs" (I'm just curious to know)? I never hear anything about those "inheritance" in the news, I wonder if anyone of them had children or any family member to reap the benefits. Maybe I need to quit "wondering so much and just do the research "huh" but then again, these are just things that whisk through my mind. I often "wonder" why we don't have many oil tycoons I'm pretty sure we were setting on top of a batch of something somewhere (some of us did get forty acres you know). I guess we are just like the Indians, too friendly and we did not know what we had and just gave it away. You know my thoughts get crazy some times, because I wonder what would have happened if Columbus had been turned away and had not been allowed to land on Plymouth Rock.

Whatever happened to "Roebuck" that used to be part of a "duo?" I wonder, whom can I "sue" for killing "Gods" little creatures that I mentioned earlier, dogs and cats are protected why not them. I even wonder, if a country is so rich (diamonds and other resources) then why are there so many poor people living in "shanty" towns, can't anyone find at least one diamond, anywhere (even I find a nickel or a dime occasionally).

If there is a deficit, I wonder why don't they just make more money, billions are being given to other countries anyway with taxpayer's money so why not? Why can't anyone see that minimum wages is the only thing that doesn't go up when gas prices, food, utilities, means of transportation and everything is inflated? I wonder what "percentage" of the prison population was receiving only minimum wages when or if they had a job, if they were trying to help their families and they did not know or did not care that they were taking the wrong approach? I wonder how many are truly remorse for the crime(s) that they committed. These are just thoughts ya'll, I'm not crazy it just things that pop up in my head.

Then I wonder why there are so many sex offenders and why they cannot control themselves. I know that I've heard many times that "sex sales" well so has the "sex offender" also but I wonder has it ever occurred to anyone that the "sex offender" doesn't want to pay for it, they just want to" steal" it, just like a robber wants to rob a bank or a car thief wants to steal a car. I "wonder" why would the authorities "warn" us to lock our cars and secure our homes to protect our "valuables", but not warn those that are walking around "barely" clothed in public you know like "thongs" or shorts so short that their cheeks are hanging out. Pubic hair would be visible also if it was not for the "wax job" that they are at risk and also might just be endangering all women, Isn't what they are exposing considered "valuable"?

When panty hose were first introduced and the skirts were raised, I assumed that was to advertise the "no seam stocking" and I thought the "new look" was kind of cute and a welcome change, from what we had to wear,(we tied our stockings in knots). I now wonder if that was a mistake and if that is when things began to get out of control. Now we have, "girls gone wild" and they're flashing "tits" on national television or any where they desire to and the mother is right there with them flashing theirs also. You can wear what you want, I am just taking you on a "tour, (my thoughts) but it seems to me that the "sex offender" could be aroused by something that they see continuously "hmm" I wonder what.

Are they "aroused" just by watching a television commercials advertising the "bikini" line being shaved that appear to look like "gestures" by the hand slowly sliding up their thigh, or "angels" walking the runway in their under wear or cheerfully "playing" with a beach ball in their underwear? It is just a thought. Could it be because the only thing covering there "valuables" while sitting on national television are their hands propped between their thighs because the skirt is so short? A mother would have taught them the proper and respectable way to sit or the "village" would have if the mother was not around (that is the way it was when we were "colored"). I wonder if it's because girls are televised talking about how much that they love having sex and the "sex" offender gets off on hearing and seeing what is "publicly" shared to the world. Some do not even wear under pants anymore I guess that is for "the booty call". Could explicit sex scenes on daytime television be the cause? I wonder why the camera operator put the camera almost in a couple's mouth just to show a kiss, does someone need kissing lesson?

It is often acknowledged that the sex offender has a "previous" criminal record and probably has an institutionalized mentality and they don't care so I wonder why no one can make the connection, who's is taunting who? I wonder why everyone can see that there are serious problems in today's time but no one seems to know how to solve them. Why is there a ticket issued for driving or riding on the passenger side without a seat belt (I always buckle up) but there in none issued for walking publicly "ass out" probably causing an accidents. I guess there were sex offenders around years ago, but in my opinion, they were not able to window shop as they do now. "Window shopping" has taken on a "new" meaning, you do not have to look in a store window any more, just step outside, and there is a variety of things to watch.

GETTING TO THE ROOT
OF THE PROBLEMS

As I previously said we can't live in the pass, but did that mean that we had to leave behind our "morals, values, and integrity"? I wonder if we were, so focus on equal opportunity or equal rights, which I will admit, was very important and long overdo, that we allowed those three "major" things to be "phased out" and we did not adjust or adapt very well. I can remember when a child wouldn't dare tell a parent or any adult to "shut up" nor would they attempt to raise their hand to" strike a parent or any adult or "roll their eyes" and a parent definitely wasn't afraid of their own child. I wonder if anyone knows what I am talking about. If that had happened, that child would have thought the rapture was upon them and would have immediately known that he or she had messed up (I can hear that child now saying, "oh, oh") because they knew that they had to face the consequences and I'm not talking about "taking a time out". Oh there would have been be a time out after you got your butt spanked, probably given extra chores, and you couldn't go outside, but guess what, back then "we were colored" and the police didn't have to get involved and there were fewer teens in jail.

I "wonder" if the authorities focused on how we raised our children during that time. "Of course" spanking is not allowed today and those that received "a lot" back then must have been some "hard heads" or "bad ass" children to keep getting whippings. I got a "switch" (a very small limb from a tree, which had the impact of a mosquito bite) on the legs one or two times and mama did not have to worry about me getting into trouble any more. That was not considered child abuse back then and as I said before, I do not ever recall seeing police roaming in the neighborhood, and there was not a need to call the authorities because children were "taught" to respect others and other people's property, "we policed our own". I wonder why I can remember the orange city bus but cannot recall what the police cars looked like or what color they were. I guess because I had to walk over a mile to the bus stop but seeing a squad car in our "neighborhood" was rare.

Well the neighborhood has changed; we now have blended communities and young teen groups trying to claim the same territory. Now the laws come in any area using "clubs, tasers, the "butt of a gun or whatever else they care to use. They beat the hell out of (your) child, slam them down to the ground to get that their "undivided attention", but a parent can't use a "switch or a belt" for the same purpose when their children are out of control at an earlier age. I "wonder," (WHAT'S THE DIFFERENCE!) and which would you rather have to deal with, a child that is taught obedience while they are still children or, a child that has become aggressive because they know that an adult can't or will not touch them "hmm"? If a child had taken something that did not belong to them or if they misbehave in any way "back then", the parent would handle it "themselves" and usually that child would learn and remember, "Not" to try that again.

The saying "it takes a village to raise a child" actually meant that back when we were "colored" an adult could handle a situation and this meant teachers also were able to discipline a student that got out of line and they had the parents' permission to do so and authorities never had to get involved. Teacher were not humiliated on the "news" while students watch and gain more power; I wonder how many people know that children are much wiser now and will take advantage of any situation every chance that they get. I wonder why is it that when we finally became "one nation", there was not a handbook issued telling us how to interact with each other, we just winged it and "all" cultures were corrupted, values and morals were lost and, I believe that is when things started changing.

It is hard to imagine a classroom with over thirty students and the teacher can't say or do anything while they are overseers except tell the student to go to the office and assume that they will go? I wonder just how 1 would handle the same situation if "I" were the teacher. I would probably pull them to the side whisper something in their ear to let them know that I do not play and it would be my word against theirs but that is why I would not teach. A teacher disciplining a student came to a complete stop, when integration started, I wonder if it was to keep certain teachers from chastising certain children. I think, parents started challenging the teachers authority in the presents of there children giving the child even "more" power.

If a student is uncontrollable in today's times, the only recourse a teacher has is to ask that student to leave the classroom, push a button that connects to the principal's office. Some schools have telephones in each classroom and some have police already in place ready to escort them off campus or take them to the juvenile detention, "that's ridiculous" police having to be assigned to schools? I wonder why everyone is trying to "pretend that they don't see what the problem is? I do not think that there would be a problem if "morals" were not been left behind and if it was not for "cultural" interference and by that, I mean, every culture had their own "methods" for disciplining their children. I'd like to know just what the "village" is suppose to do when they have to watch what they say, be very careful about what they do and overlook what they see or hear because of fear of being attacked by a child, arrested by the authorities or ostracized by their peers if their decisions aren't approved.

In my opinion, the "new" village is not reaching the majority, they're only scratching the surface and hand picking who to save even though they say, "no" child left behind when there is an epidemic situation that is happening and it's getting worse each day. Prayer was an important part of our schools "back then" but it was removed when we became one nation under "God" (another word phased out) and I think one person was responsible for that. I do not know if all schools even had prayer but it was acceptable, where I came from and it was how we started our day. You know I often wonder if all schools allowed prayer then, that is something, you do not think of when you are a child but now, I wonder. I remember when everyone stopped whatever they were doing when "The National Anthem" was playing and for the reciting of "Prayer and the Pledge of Allegiance", (all of that's gone now) and you know I will bet many of today's children are not even aware that this is what was done. Nowadays some kids have very little respect for anything and they hardly fear anyone (now that is deep).

If a child was involved in any activities, there was at least one parent there for moral support and more thrilled about seeing a parent in the audience rooting for them than they were focused on what they were doing and even if they made a mistake, mom or dad showed no signs of disappointment. The children were given a treat, maybe just going to eat out on a school night to celebrate their accomplishments or attempts. Teen parties were always chaperoned with at least two adults (not any more). Now we have the "news age" parent and I wonder why some of them cannot control their children. Is it because they just don't know how or are they afraid that the authorities might charge them with something if the child tells there side and again I say "time out doesn't work" on every child especially after they reach a certain age and what is the cut off age for that anyway.

Now some of my thoughts come from things mentioned to the public and as children got older, parents thought that being "buddies" would work better than being a parent would. They started partying with together, going to the clubs with them, smoking or drinking alcohol with them, allowing them to engage in sex in the house because that's one way that they could keep an eye on their child. A parent use to almost always know whom their daughters were dating and there was no such thing as, running out to get in a car after hearing the "honk of a horn", the young man would have to come to the door. Entertaining in the bedroom was definitely out of the question, and they did not just leave home without their parent's knowledge. A child would not say," I'll be back after while" without some sort of explanation as to where they were going. They might not have told the truth about where they were going but the question was asked and a child would think twice when they were out how they carried themselves because the "village" was always on patrol and "snitching" was acceptable then. I not trying to say that everyone was a saint, simply stating that there was more adult control, they were the authority and not the law (now that's what I remember).

Whether or not a child was born out of wedlock in the past, the mother usually knew whom the baby's daddy was. I wonder how a mother cannot know the father of their child. I could possibly understand testing maybe two people, but to test ten or more people is ludicrous, please, give me a break. I wonder how long does ovulation last, is it a whole month or is there a sign at their door saying open for business twenty four seven anyone is welcome? I really would like to know and I wonder if there was a retest, would the results be the same? Are guys carrying a spare cotton swab from someone else and possibly made a "switch" (just a thought) some people are "slick as okra" and could pull a fast one but I'm no expert.

Our Family Police Department

(From left to right) Deputies, Uncle Ed, my Mama Sallie Norman, Uncle Jim, Aunt Lota, Uncle Arthur, Aunt Hester, assistant chief of police, my grand mother Mama McCullough, and Chief of Police Arthur "Daddy" McCullough. (Below) John Arthur Norman Jr. (my father) was head person in charge of our household. That is all we needed to stay in line (I forgot the village).

A child needs to know their parents this is one of the most important factors in their development. They need love, protection; guidance, understanding, acknowledgement for good deeds, and most all, they need "Jesus". Let me repeat this again, if you say "ouch" then that is whom I am referring to.

Now what you read from this point is just my analogy of what the "root" of today's problems are. First, let me go on record to say we were not all saints and there were fights back then. There were sticks used to swing at someone rarely ever hitting anyone, and rocks thrown, I even saw knives and ice picks used, but I had never seen a murder or serious gangs and I have no idea where all of the guns came from "hmm". Now adults just look the other way probably out of fear of what might happen to them. I also want to reiterate that the parent and the village are no longer as strong as they use to be. Maybe because some are afraid to interfere with a child's behavior without fear of getting in trouble or getting hurt themselves and young people feel with confidence that he or she cannot be touched; they now have gained "the power". Keep in mind also that this is "reality writing" and if you have read this part before, it is like everything else that is happening in this time, "anything goes" and almost "everything" is accepted.

I do not know if it is because the authorities took over or if it is just the new way of parenting or not, but from what I have "observed", that seems to be when the floodgates were opened, and the prison systems became big business. The sad thing about this new age generation is, they are very intelligent but they do not know how to channel their capabilities. They have been exposed to more adult activities by the age ten than I knew after I had been married and had children. Too much freedom is allowed to a child and some are very belligerent and demanding. I have "observed" that some teens started trying to outdo each other with "over priced" tennis shoes. I wonder if "super stars" can take part of the blame after all they are the ones that reap the benefits and the child after standing in line might only have the shoes for a day before someone steals them or they just might get killed for them. I wonder if it is because "rappers" that became famous after they had been "incarcerated" wear expensive and usually "excessive" amount of jewelry. Some for selling drugs or maybe they were affiliated with a gang and they "boast" about their battle wounds that they received, or pimps that also became "successful" and continuously support (pimp) conventions I guess because nowadays as it is said and I "quote" it's hard out there being a pimp and they need a spokes person.

I wonder what is the purpose of owning "over priced" purses and do not even have a dime to put in them. Now we have a rivalry started between the haves and the have not's. I wonder if the gangs that are formed started from the have not's and what they are trying to achieve and are they motivated by everything that has been "glamorized"

While sitting here writing down my thought's, a very gruesome murder has occurred, a young man killed his girlfriend then cut her up and then burned her body the reason given by one of the murderer's family was he was "abandoned" by his parent's. I am trying to end this journey but there's not a day that goes by that I can watch the news and not see corruption all around, sex is exploited and now wedding days aren't sacred any more, if you want "suggestive" photos for your husband "eyes only", then why am I able to see it, why is it televised? Just do it!! Police cars and yellow crime scene tapes are roping off some areas every day. Kids are rounded up like cattle for crimes committed but no one is trying to get inside their heads to figure out if there is a problem but I guess you have to be rich and famous to get a mental evaluation. I would love to know each child that is behind bars life story.

I'm willing to bet that poor parenting or abuse of some kind played a big part in their life or they want what has been "glamorized" by the ones that they look up to and think that's prison is the only way to make it to the big times. I am sure there is a story within each one of them, my grandson has one and he is the reason that I took this journey and this is his story.

THE BEST INSTITUTION FOR HIGHER LEARNING

State Correctional University (S.C.U.)

The Breeding Factory

The Best Institution for Higher Learning

State Correctional University (S.C.U.)

This institution has many curriculums and one might enroll only with one "topic" (offense) but graduate with many. Most colleges or universities are mostly four year terms but S.C.U is even better, ten to twenty or however long the "people in charge" determine that your studies should be now that's a long time to learn. Now S.C.U is not an institution that I would recommend to anyone but it is very easy to enroll. You don't have to have S.A.T. scores, financial aid nor do you need to apply for a student loan. Parents do not have to refinance their homes for the tuition unless they hire a professional (attorney) to assist them with their studies; (most already paid when they were not allowed to or was afraid to discipline their children) "it's free except for your "tax dollars". To qualify for S.C.U., you only need one of the following, very low self esteem, neglect from parents (abuse, mental or physical), have been bullied by a class mate, under peer pressure (wanting acceptance from losers) or easily be influenced by things that's been "glamorized". The average age of admission to the S.C.U. begins at seventeen or eighteen and by that age, some have already been to the "junior college version" J.D.C. (juvenile detention center) and think that they are prepared for S.C.U.

Once you are admitted, then you are an "institutionalize" slave. You are issued a uniform that is mandatory and the colors are usually bright orange or black and white stripes depending on which university that you attend.

You are told when to get up when to go to bed and you might have to do "push ups" totally naked just for a routine "body" count or if someone causes trouble whether or not you were involved and the hall monitors (guards) get a "free" show (now how cool is that). Since they (guards) request this show I wonder if they just want to get their "freak" on, now these are some of the things that in my journey I've been made aware of. I forgot to mention that these "distinctive" institutions are located all over the U.S . . . Try to imagine how many students enrolled, it has to be an overwhelming number. Your dormitory (cell) is very large usually twenty five to thirty classmates (inmates), per class and they are also your "slash" study partners (isn't that just great) you get to collaborate with each other (that's when you first enroll). You have to rely on your "hired" professor's (lawyers), to try to get you through the course as quickly as possible. If he is good at his profession, he might be able to get you a mental evaluation but then again you would need to have money for that. It is somewhat sad though because if you were important, then you would have a cakewalk and not the "child be that was left behind" that was abused in some way but I forget, if you are enrolled already, then you are not a child anymore.

Back to what I was talking about, I kind of got sidetrack for a moment just thinking. There is know privacy to take care of personal hygiene, the toilet is in an open area so that everyone can see you take care of your business, I wonder why that is shown in the television "series" they show everything else. You have to eat with your classmates (inmates), so therefore you can share with each other's ideas. You exchange notes on "how to" or figure out what went wrong so they will know what not to do when they have completed their term at S.C.U. You get a smaller room with just one roommate if you are a long-term student, which means that your "hired" professor was not as good as you would have liked him to be.(Don't get discourage though because you might be one of the lucky ones).

Your roommate just might have been there long enough to be working on his or her P.H.S.O. (pedophile, Homosexual, and Sex Offender) degree and not being able to have any physical contacts and you being a freshman means that you are now also the "apprentice" until they graduate (released). Isn't that just great, now that you have "pledged" involuntarily, you have a new "subject" added to your curriculum to work on your "masters". It has been said, that if you feed someone garbage long enough then it begins to taste like steak and if you keep a dog chained to a post that dog will become more aggressive when it has turned loose. That same theory applies to someone that is humiliated by having to expose everything that they do in front of twenty or thirty classmates or their roommate so they just get to where they just do not give a darn. Now I ask you," who's really the dumb ones, the classmates or the overseers"? (My thoughts, my journey)

Now some of them realize that they made the wrong school choice but once you are accepted, you might have to wait years before you graduate. When you have completed all of the courses, you will probably have a "Masters Degree" in criminology. Some enroll dumb and graduate dumber with the fact overlooked that you were abused in some way before you entered S.C.U . . . While you were enrolled there your classmate or the person abused you probably over the class (the jailer). When you leave S.C.U. you are ostracized from society, you can't find work, and you are looked upon as scum, you can't vote so there's nothing left but to fall back on the subjects that you learned while at S.C.U. (isn't that just wonderful).

Now there is a different criteria for the "rich and the famous", it does not really matter what they do (drunk driving, vehicular manslaughter, drug possession, money laundering), even murder apparently they must have gotten a short-term scholarships "they are the smarter ones". There is no classmate assigned to them, well maybe one because their dormitory only can hold only two people (more privacy). I guess they are quick learners because they whiz through their term with ease; maybe they get a warning or forty days (that time might be reduced) but no more than two years. If you are a "famous celebrity", there is no time served at all for "indecent exposure", they can show all of their "valuables" to the world and that is considered "news" but if you are an "unknown" and do the same thing then it is considered "prostitution" or "indecent exposure" and you will be "enrolled" immediately. I wonder why the photographer is not considered a "pervert" but is paid for the shots.

Now everyone was not born with a "silver spoon" in their mouth or achieved celebrity status but God gave everyone a "gift". "To me" it would make more sense and be more practical to find out from the "less fortunate ones" who's true capabilities are unknown when they were admitted as teenagers (just babies), just what their "true" attributes are, try to develop that "God given" talent so they could be more productive in society in a positive way. Close your eyes for a moment and just imagine all of the overcrowded prisons all over the United States, then ask yourself this question, {how many scientist, mathematicians, historians, musicians, artist and politicians "they lie a lot you know" "etc" are behind bars?} "Hmmm" Their "gifts" were probably overlooked, laugh at, or a parent thought that their dreams were ridiculous. They had ideas of what they wanted to become in life, they might have been exceptional in their quest but just did not have the resources or have anyone to see the potentials in them and they became frustrated.

Again I say when we were "colored", S.C.U. was not over crowded with our youth because we would disciplined "our" children, the neighbors or any adult could discipline "our" children, the teachers most definitely could discipline "our" children because the village wasn't in the class room and neither was the parent and the teacher had the entire class by themselves. In my opinion, the reason for this "over crowded" situation at S.C.U. is, we came together "as one" but we didn't "sit down" together to discuss just how each cultures handled situations, there wasn't a handbook issued to one another explaining the dos and don'ts, we just abided by "one set of principles" other people's rules and regulations. We knew how to handle "our" own children but those rights were taken away.

You know what really amazes me. How things are justified in some cases while others are just cut and dry, for an example, a "repeated" offender, (not sex or murderers) is not "diagnosed" as having a problem so they go untreated, just considered a menace to society, and need to be put away for years. On the other hand, a person can "repeatedly" kill child after child and is "diagnosed" as having some sort of disorder. A "fifteen" year old already "traumatized" because she is pregnant and suffering "mentally" feeling the guilt of what she had done fatally to her new born child didn't get "professional" help she merely carried the "burden" inside, received six years in prison as punishment, while the wealthy receives only a hand slap for butchering someone. Her suffering will last a lifetime and it makes me "wonder" just how many of you that has judged her, how many of you that do not have any "skeletons" and can cast the first stone.

DON'T JUST CAGED THE MIND, REFURBISH IT

"Turn a negative into a positive"

A billionaire made a comment on national television that we need more youth interested in "math and science" there just aren't enough young people who care. I have to disagree with that statement, there is an "abundance" of sapient (full of knowledge) minds, with abilities to do great things, but they are either locked up behind bars or they are being killed in a war that was not ours to begin with. Just imagine if someone putting as much effort in a young person "locked up" as they do finding ways to get richer or going clear across the world to adopt a child to "create" a new image (remember the rock). "Example" give one of them a challenge of assembling something that you might consider complicated or problems difficult to solve maybe even a draw a portrait of something that you pay someone" thousands of dollars" to draw and see what the outcome will be. Does anyone know how richer this country could become if people "with the power" could recognize that what we need "economically" is right here in this country and they could give "back" to the community but no one wants to take the time or the chance to "tap" into a "potential" goldmine. (My thoughts)

Here is a little story within a story. There was a choir director searching for a musician because she could not play a "lick" and the church could not "afford" to pay very much. The word was out there on the streets as to what she needed, in the clubs, the beer joints and the hole in the wall.

Only one person took the offer saying that he would do it and he had not ever played in a church before. The director picked him up one Sunday morning for church because he didn't even have a car and the first thing that he mentioned was, he was an addict I guess that was to let her know in case she wanted to change her mind or he slipped up. She then asked him, "Can you play" he chuckled and replied yes I can and her response was, her job was to find a musician and it's God's job to clean you up. There were some rough patches; times when he didn't show up because of his addiction but the director persevered through his struggle taking him to rehab, clinics, and the work source because what she had found, was a "diamond" in the rough. His drug dealers (wannnabe rappers) also knew his capabilities and took advantage of his gift. He had a college degree and he could just hear a song and was able to it play to "perfection in ten minutes and also chart a song on paper in no time. It did not take to long because with patience and of course "God", he has been clean for over eight years. The moral to this little story is everyone can change with a little help.

To all of you scholars, decision makers, leaders, and "attention" getters, try using this analogy, "the computer". I hope that all of you know that man was not the creator of the computer, God was. Let us just call the human body a "case", and in this case, is the brain that we will call "the mother board" now think about this, at *S.C.U.*, the "case" and the "mother board" are already (incarcerated) and they are just sitting there "dormant" with nothing to do but wait for time served. Now I ask "all" of you to take this challenge, since there are "millions" of computer parts (inmates) all over this country attending *S.C.U.* some with memory already installed (inventors, historians, mathematicians, architect, artist, etc), to try building on them. Since you already have the resource and the finances to do so, then why not invest in adding more RAM "memory" to add to the "mother board" or the hard drive "the brain" instead of letting their classmates (other inmates) program negative memory into them,"? "YOU HAVE THE POWER" so make this country, better, richer and "less" violent. Take these young minds and enhance what is already there before their minds become further corrupted and, "institutionalized". Most of these "young" people are there simply because of ignorance, they were abandoned by a parent, some are frustrated because they cannot read or write past a third grade level and maybe because they "crave attention" from their parents, they "lashed" out at the world. I "guarantee" that you will see an improvement in our country that will "benefit" everyone, and be more "profitable" to you (you will like that). If you use the money that you spend on building more "prisons", try adding a wing onto the already existing (prisons) and have them equipped with "secured" classrooms "not the "traditional" types because that's what landed them there in the first place. Build classrooms with specific "curriculums" best suited for their God given gifts "first", then add a little reading and writing and refurbish their minds (it's like going in through the back door) remember, their "gifts" first then books. Include also a "psychiatrist" to analyze "each" individuals level of learning.

All of you "super stars" that have made lots of money off "overpriced" tennis shoes and jerseys that these young people probably stole to have. Rappers" who made crime appear to be a gateway to success flashing your jewelry and your "brass teeth" which youth try to simulate. Pimps" that "glorify" marketing in their own words, "bitches and whores" or "drug dealers" that "flash" money "tempting" young people to "work" for you; I ask all of you to take this challenge along with the "other" rich and famous people. Since there are "millions" of computer parts (inmates) all over this country attending S.C.U. some with memory already installed (inventors, historians, mathematicians, architect, artist, etc), to build on them. You all have the money and some of you helped "contribute", taking them into the homes of the "rich and famous" some of you know how you got there and so does the inmate because you told them. If you just "try" this approach, it will create more jobs for teachers with specialties, build better mind for the future of inmates so that there will be less "violence" (probably by seventy five percent) on the streets when they've completed there "term" at S.C.U.

If this country can spend a "Billion" dollars to aid another country, (heard it on the news) and eight hundred million of that cannot be "accounted for; we can "scrap" projects gone wrong spending millions of "tax payer" dollars. Let's not forget poor old "Sojourner", she's lost in space somewhere I believe on Mars; then why can't we "invest" in making our country safer after all we have "lost" a lot of good people trying to help other countries to be safe. Make S.C.U. a training base for those not yet "institutionalized" before it is too late.

"TAKE THE CHALLENGE"!

I dare you.

I am inserting this poem of inspiration not just to promote the poet (my son) but to reach souls

The Fisher of Men
By Norris Williams II

This is a little story
About a fisher of men
Who fishes for the sinners
Then tries to reel them in MAT 4:18-22

To get them on his hook
He has to use the right bait
The bait of love and kindness
God says "That's all it takes" 1 PET 1: 22-25

When he gets them in the church
And he fills them with God's word
He is building up their faith
To preach the things they've heard ACT 20:32-38

After he's filled then with God's word
And stripped them of flesh and sin
He deploys the back to the world
To reel more sinners in ROM 7-7-25

He is fighting a war with Satan
Who will steal, kill and destroy
But the mighty mission of the fisher
Is to reel, fill, and deploy JN 10: 1-29

MY GRANDSON'S STORY

His mother and father (my son) dated in high school. His father received both academic and athletic scholarships. I do not know the reason, but they broke up and my son moved on with his life and was in the second half of his first year of college and she graduated a year or so later. His dad's grades were good that year so he started dating someone new. He came home from school one weekend with his new girlfriend so that I could meet her and for some reason my daughter felt the need to call his ex-girlfriend and tell her that her brother was home. That is when she decided to come and "announce" that he was going to be a father. That caused confusion between him and his girlfriend so they broke it up. He then dropped out of college to get a job to take care of his responsibilities.

One week after my grandson was born; his mother brought him over for his father to baby-sit (which meant me also) while she went "Christmas" shopping (can you believe that?). That shopping spree lasted almost a week, and while in our care, his navel cord came off while I was changing him. About two months later the phone calls started coming almost every weekend, my son was threatened with the thought of never seeing his child if he didn't keep him on any particular weekend that she didn't feel like being bothered with him (her on child). I remember hearing my son say to her, 'I kept him last weekend', I could hear the abusive language over the phone the name calling such as "fat ass", motherf—r and all that I didn't hear, I was told what was said like the threat that he would never see his child again. To keep down confusion I told him to tell her to bring him over after all we had no legal rights since my son name was not on the birth certificate and he did not want to lose contact with his son so he complied with her demands. He had no experience with childcare but he did the best that he could, I helped after all, this was my "first" grandchild and I knew there were some things that his dad was not quite comfortable doing (bathing him and changing diapers).

I remember one weekend his mom brought the baby over and left so quickly, she did mentioned that he had a cold but she left before I realized that he was burning up with a fever. Thank God that I had aspirins, they were not baby aspirins so I had to improvise breaking the aspirin in half and give him a small portion of that half and held him all night while he slept just to make sure he would be all right. There was no way to contact her I tried but I guess she had not made it home yet or she just was not answering her phone. Back then, cell phones were not that popular I am talking about in the 80's, I could not take him to the emergency room because we were not legal guardians but all turned out well because the fever did finally break by morning. I wonder if CPS would have charged me with interfering if they knew. I have no idea who kept him those times that he was not with us while his mother was at work. When he became old enough to attend daycare, his mother asked me if she could place my name on the list as the responsible person to pick him up some evenings even though the daycare was clear across town and closer to her family. Of course, I said yes after all, this is my "first" grandson and I made sure that he was not there after hours because she (his mom) would have to pay late charge. I did not really make the connection at the time, but it was usually on a Friday that she would call for me to pick him up and I will admit that I was elated that I would have my grandson on the weekend. At some point back then, we ended up keeping him "every weekend"; now keep in mind, my son and his mom were no longer dating. His (grandson) mom had a very abusive boyfriend and one day, she came to our home seemingly panic stricken. Constantly looking over her shoulder saying that her boyfriend had tried to run her and my grandson off the road, well we told her to stay until she calmed down and of course we thought we were ready for him if he had followed her. Looking back on that situation, we had no weapons because we are a "non-violent" family, I do not know what we were going to do but I knew we were not going to let him hurt my "only" grandchild. They were safe for a moment, he had not followed them and then again, she could have been lying about the whole thing.

I remember a phone call from his mom and there was panic in her voice and I also heard a very obnoxious loud voice in the background I gave the phone to my son to find out what was going on apparently there was some sort of abuse happening and he immediately called "911" and told them about the situation. The police met him at her apartment because he wanted to get his son out of harm's way. They (the police) asked her about the disturbance and what did she want them to do? Everything had calmed but the boyfriend boldly was still there, since the authorities had been called they asked her if she'd allow the baby to leave with his father and she said yes, to me this was an opportunity for her to also have her boyfriend removed. Just imagine the trauma my grandson must have experienced at such a young and formative age and he had not even started kindergarten yet. While in our care she allowed us enroll him in the daycare close to our home at "our" expense, I did not complain. after all when he was with her, she never ask for child support so I didn't complain about paying the fees although she didn't have to ask because we made sure he was well taken care of and not neglected in anything, this was probably our weakness and boy did she really take advantage of that. We showered him with gifts when he was a baby, for birthdays and Christmas, all holidays, or just because we saw something we wanted him to have after all this was my "first" grandson and my son's only child.

When he was old enough to attend kindergarten which is "free" (well he really wasn't old enough) she falsified his birth certificate so that he could enroll a year ahead of schedule to avoid paying for daycare, she "his mother" decided that she would keep him, and she still had the "abusive" boyfriend. His after school babysitter must have been Hispanic, the reason I say this is because when he was with us on weekends. He would run to the door and yell as loud as he could, "911, repeatedly "911". He could say it in Spanish "Nueve Uno Uno" well at first I just thought it was funny and was thinking at the time how smart that he was but while laughing at him doing that, the phone rang, I answered and it was "911" calling to find out if someone had called. That is when it hit me that my grandchild had learned how to call the police and being a kid he was playing on the phone and was having a "practice drill" because obviously he was in no danger with us. I often wondered what all he had endured while in her care. Well she kept him through kindergarten and first grade (he was only five years old in the first grade but very smart and he caught on quickly) apparently his mom did not recognize that she had a gifted child.

I cannot recall the reason, but she allowed him to stay with us in the second grade "probably to avoid after school day care fees". Since he was staying with us now, we enrolled him in the same school that his father attended not to far our home and while his father was at work, I would pick him up after school. One day while sitting in my car in front of the school, waiting for him to run out like he normally did, I noticed the crowd of children were thinning out. He had not come out yet so I went to the office to see where he was, I was informed that his mother had picked him up without our knowledge. I guess she and my son had exchanged words with each other and she wanted to send us a message that she was the dominant parent. He grew up during the time when "marriage" no longer had meaning so going back and forward between parents was normal. This time he must have sensed danger because that same evening we got a phone call, it was him it was the first chance that he got to sneak and called us and in his voice I detected fear, I was also fearful because I didn't know where she lived. I told him to look at the numbers on the house and let me know what it read. He was one-step ahead of me he had notice things on the way to where she had taken him and said to me "granny", you know that store with the big bird on the front, I am close to that place in some apartments. For a six year old, his navigation skills were good and again I ask him to give me an address if he could; he did not know the numbers but he did know the name of the apartments "Beechnut Place Two" not the name of the street which was probably the same and he had details about the gate.

Apparently he did not like the situation that he was in and wanted us to come and get him he but we had no legal rights because his dad's name was never placed on the birth certificate. His dad didn't panic he just calmly said, "Mama" she's not going to keep him" because that meant she would have to take off from work to enroll him in school where she lived' and "pay" someone to keep him after school. I was not quite convinced that she would bring him back but even if she did not, we did not have a "legal" leg to stand on, of course he was right she brought him back the very next day, she had made her point. He did complete his second year of school "stress free" living with us. His mother decided that she would keep him his third year of school which was clear across town, we really did not have a say in what she did (we thought) so we had to comply and it was back to keeping him on weekends. By then we had truly bonded with him and we did not hesitate to keep him any chance we got.

He completed that year living with his mother and her abusive boyfriend then she ask us to pick him up from school on the last day and of course we were so excited to see him we were there early waiting for the bell to ring. We thought we were to have him for a week, but as it turned out, we kept him the entire summer, she was back to her old usual self again and actually, I was glad that she was because my grandbaby had an un-explained scar on his leg and I did not want him out there anymore. At the end of summer, I guess his mother had gotten use to the freedom from paying babysitters and the fear of being caught allowing him to be a latch-key kid at such a young age, so she decided to let him stay with us his fourth year of elementary school. She waited until the last minute to let us know and it was too late to enroll him in the same school he had gone to when he was with us in his second year it was full.

Even though he loved his mother very much, he felt safe and secure with us and was glad to be able to go to school while living with us. We had to try to find a school closes to where we lived, and the closes one was in a very low poverty area. I would not have mind but some of the parents were extremely ignorant. Some would come to pick up their children in "scanty" clothing that only their husband or boyfriend should see them in, they were hollering at their children down the hallway or outside with foul language that shouldn't be heard by anyone. I had to get him out of that school, it took three weeks but we finally found another school in the area that would accept him. He was adjusting very well in his new surroundings and when I visited the school for a progress report, I was very impressed by the teacher's comments. The teacher said that my grandson was extremely smart just like he was when he in school I chuckled a little bit. I knew he meant it and I was so proud of how my grandson focused. The teacher then told me that he had to place my him at a table by himself with lots of work to keep him busy because the class was a little to slow for him, his homework was done before he got home he was very anxious.

That year he won the "spelling bee" in his classroom and then represented his school in the citywide competition, where he placed fifth competing with students ranging from forth to ninth grade. He had called his mother to tell her that he had won the school competition and wanted her to come to the semi-finals, you could see the disappointment as he looked all over the audience, but she didn't show up. I will never forget the word that he miss-spelled it was "benevolent' I know had he taken his time, he would have won easily. He then asked tearfully, granny "how come my mama didn't come she said that she was going to come". I painfully told him even though I really did not know why, that she probably could not get off from work and he said with anger, "she just lied to me". At that point, I really did not know what to say to him and my mind just drifted I guess to block out our feelings I reminisced on when I was a child; we couldn't even say the word lie in front of mama. Can you believe that is what popped up in my mind?

His teacher suggested and I realized that my grandson needed to be in a school that challenged his intellect, so I had a talk with his mother explaining what the teacher and I thought was best for him and she agreed. I explained to her that I wanted to take him out of the public school system and place him in a private "Christian" school because he had a gift and at that time, there were only eight students per class. I explained to her how much it cost and asked her if she would be willing to pay half, of course she agreed but did not give one dime. I enrolled him any way it was a strain on the budget but it was worth every penny. At this school, your child was not allowed to leave out and run to the car when school was out each day, a responsible person had to come in and get their child, most of the time it was me, his gray haired grandmother. Even though I knew that he was not ashamed of me, I also knew that he would have loved his mother to come and get him so that his classmates could see her. One day I called her to suggest that she come and visit him at school sometimes, I guess she must have sensed the anger in my voice. She surprisingly gave him a birthday party in his classroom I had to meet her in the parking lot because the school was in a business district and she did not have a clue where to go.

We found out his strongest subjects was mathematics and computers. He was so gifted in math that his teacher let him tutor some of his classmates, I was so proud of my grandson. Realizing his ability to grasp things quickly, I then decided to let him take piano lessons, he learned the notes on the keyboard with ease; I had to tell him to slow down because he was not taking time to learn the theory of music, which is very important. The lessons were only forty dollars a month, which was a good rate. Although he was now living with us, he loved his mother so much and he would look forward to the weekends waiting for her to come and pick him up. He would call her with much excitement to see what time she was going to come and then say to me," Granny my mama "(gone) come get me this weekend" and I would respond "that's great" of course he waited and waited, he would stand at the front door looking down the street but she never came. The disappointing expression on his face trying to hold back the tears just tore me up inside each time.

During that year close to the end of school, he was playing and he fell and got a gash in the back of his head that required stitches, they used clamps instead, thank God, his father had insurance coverage on his job for him. Well, summer came, school was out his mother did come to get him to spend some time with her. I explain to her that he was taking music lessons and all she had to do was take him on Saturdays, the lessons were already paid and she was also told about the clamps in his head and she would have to take him to have them removed when it was time since he was with her. She assured me that she would but she did not take him to one lesson her reason was, he said that he did not want to go. That was unbelievable because he was doing so well and looked forward to going. She was still with her abusive boyfriend after all this time and little did I know at the time she was still allowing her boyfriend to abuse him. Well summer was over, she returned him back to us, and he was so happy because he knew he was home. I asked him did he have a good time, he was somewhat reserved but he said, "It was alright". She did not take him to get his hair cut so I did not notice at first, but I soon discovered that she had not taken him to have the clamps removed from the back of his head, was I furious. We took him to a Medic Stop Clinic and to hear him scream when they removed the clamps was heart wrenching.

He was now a fifth grader at the same private school and again she would not pay her half of the tuition but that was okay I had only asked her once. The school always had "project assignments", all of the students had to write a poem, and each poem was going to be submitted for selection to be placed in the 2000 edition of the "Young Poets speak out". Once again, he had an accomplishment; his poem was one out of many chosen, (two from each grade level). He called his mom to tell her the good news in fact every time that he achieved something, he wanted his mother to know about it and be proud of him but she showed no signs of caring. He loved her so much and did everything that he could that was positive hoping that she would show signs of caring but nothing that he accomplished seemed important to her.

The next year, the school was having a Mother's Day Brunch inviting all mothers. The school staff knew me but was not sure if his mother would attend since they had only seen her once so his teacher gave him two invitations to be on the safe side. We didn't want him to be disappointed, well I called his mom and told her if she didn't show up that time, then she have to deal with me I don't know how but I was just trying to make sure that she would come, needless to say my threat must have worked because she showed up. While attending school there, he was basketball team; his mother never attended a game. He played little league baseball (first base was his position), he also played little league football (he was the quarterback) his dad was the coach and still his mother never went to any game.

After picking him up from school one day while driving home, I remember so well how extremely quiet he was and 1 looked over at him and noticed he had tears in his eyes and he was trembling so I ask him, baby what's wrong? His reply was, "I don't know why my mama don't want me" and 1 had to find away to hold back my tears and assure to him that she did 1 can still hear him saying that just like it was yesterday. He was a good child and tried to excel in everything that he did. There was the time I took him to youth choir rehearsal with me, I was the director and I ask one of the children to lead us in prayer and without hesitation he said, "I'll do it granny".

Well I was surprised when he said that and was expecting a quickie prayer from him and we all bowed our heads with eyes close he began to pray. About a minute into his prayer, I had to peek because he was still praying. I told him after rehearsal how proud I was of him for volunteering and he said with a smile Granny "you didn't know I could do that huh"?

There were many fun times but there was the pain that he was carrying deep inside that he just could not let go. His six-grade year was the year all hell broke loose, everything was uncovered. His mother had gotten married (not to the abusive boyfriend thank God) and had gotten everything for her house and I guess she didn't need us anymore and thought he was old enough to stay home by himself, my daughter heard from someone that she was about to make her move and take him from us. I told you at the beginning, my son's name was never put on the birth certificate and legally she could come and get him anytime that she wanted, and we wouldn't be able to stop her remember? Well 1 was one step ahead of her; I got an attorney to fight for legal custody, 1 told my lawyer the story of how we'd had him most of his life, but there's a part that 1 left out of this story until now. In the beginning when I first laid eyes on my grandson, whom I love dearly, I said to my son, "this is not your baby". My daughter made the comment," there she goes again (speaking of me), she think she knows everything and of course my son being a proud dad agreed with his sister so I just left it alone and said nothing else, well every now and then I'd mention it but not in front of my grandbaby of course. Back then, people weren't really getting tested because it was assumed that whenever a women said who the father was then, usually that's who it was.

His mother had been served with papers in an attempt to gain legal custody of him and naturally she challenged us. She made threatening phone calls letting us know we were not getting her child and in her own words she said, "We'll see who gets him in court", I'm his mother". I wasn't fazed by her comment after all I had him most of his life and in my possession are medical records, S.A.T. scores, TAAS test results, awards, trophies, etc.. We all had our attorney, she had hers, and there was one for my grandson also she then realized we were serious about getting custody and not intimidated by the fact that she was his mother my son knew that being his father, he had rights also. She then begged us not to take her son from her but what she didn't understand is, we didn't want to lose him either after all she practically gave him to us, cursing and making threatening remarks that he'd never see his son again, calling him to come to "her" rescue because his was in danger, remember?

The attempts that she made to try to get her child were a little too late and her last effort was telling the courts the truth, my son was "not" the father. The three were ordered to have D.N.A. testing, this was all happening around his twelfth birthday; his father and I knew that if we had waited until then, there was nothing we could do. Our lawyer called and said Mrs. Williams you were right, I ask right about what? She said the D.N.A. results are in and your son is not his father. I was not surprise but I was devastated knowing the pain he and his father were feeling but what hurt us the most was the fact that she knew even before he was born that my son was "not" his biological father. Knowing the truth did not stop the love that we had because we are a family and she thought that knowing the truth, we would let her have custody without a fight.

He was now twelve and could decide where he wanted to live and was ask to sign an affidavit to make his choice. He chose his dad that was a decision I am sure that he dreads having to make because even though she had never been there for him, he truly loved his mother and he did not want her to be angry with him. The person that he felt secure with was the only father that he knew; he had not been around her long enough to feel comfortable living with her so he chose his father.

His mother thought we had coerced him into signing and she insisted that he do it again and he made the same choice I cannot imagine how he must have felt having to make a choice. This enraged her and that is when his life started spiraling downward. She began calling asking to speak to "her child" only to curse him trying to make him feel worse than he already felt. It was so bad one time and so loud, that my daughter and I could hear her and before I could reach for the phone, my daughter took the phone away from my grandson. His tears began to flow and I cannot even imagine the pain he was feeling it had to be unbearable because I know the pain I was feeling. Believe me, if he wanted to live with his mother, we would not have pressured him to stay with us the decision was all his and we made sure he understood that. Although he loved his mother very much he also knew without a doubt that he was loved and had stability with us and we would never make him feel unwanted, he knew that he was at home and he did not have to ask for simple things like "could he get something out of the refrigerator".

When her attorney found out that she had lied for twelve years, and he knew it was not going to be open and shut, he requested to be removed from the case. She then hired another attorney and then all three attorneys (hers, his) and ours went into mediation before the judge. After they heard his mom history, how she was never really in his life, and she nothing tangible of his to show that he had lived with her, my attorney stepped out of the mediation to tell us this is a "slam dunk case" and she did not stand a chance in hell of getting her own son.

We went to court and after the judge heard the details of the case, my son and I were awarded legal custody and, she was ordered to pay child support, and was given visitation rights, we didn't even ask for back pay for the twelve years we were just glad it was over (we thought). She very seldom took advantage of her rights, her new husband would come and get him on the designated visit but on the weekday visitations, she was at work and he did not get to spend with her. Her husband had a daughter, I cannot say whether or not that she lived with them but my grandson observed that she felt more at home there than he did. He felt badly because he really loved her and wanted her desperately to love him in return; he just did not know her well enough to feel comfortable living with her all the time. He told me about the time when they were supposed to go to the store, he was excited and was looking forward to the trip. To him that was "quality time" that he would spend with his mom but that dream was shattered when she told her step-daughter to come and ride with them and insisted that he sit in the back seat, "wow" that was a blow to him. He expressed to her that it was all right. He did not want to go any more and of course, he was verbally abused for his action.

Thinking of his mother always brought him to tears and he always wanted to know why she did not want him or love him.

He became unruly one day in his class, not for fighting anyone but for horseplay when the teacher had left the room. There was zero tolerance so he had to leave the private school. We knew then that he seriously needed professional help to try to get him through all the devastation. His father and I sought psychiatric help for him, we attended nine sessions with him, and every time he was asked about his mother, he would break down cry, so it was easy for the psychiatrist to know what the root of his problem was. His mother was also ask to attend nine sessions, she only attended one claiming it was a waste of time and the office was too far.

It was a "culture" shock for him to go back to public school because the classes had more than twice the amount of students that he was use to and some of them didn't seem to be as focus on class work like he was accustom to so because he had "rejection" issues, he tried to fit in. His desire to learn had dissipated, and even though he wanted acceptance by his peers he persevered striving to do his best in his classes hoping that she would be proud of him, he was really juggling himself. He was a candidate for "Who's Who" of America's high school students; he was in all advanced classes and was still helping some of his classmates. He did okay academically even though his G.P.A. had dropped under three point zero, he maintained a two point eight. He "always" attended classes, was liked by his teachers, he never slammed a door or raised his voice to anyone "except" on the football field when he slammed his helmet to the ground. I believe that was the only time that he had released all of his frustration that he was holding inside; he was the "quarterback" and was angry when there was a bad play.

Although we never missed a game, his mother never came to any and that disappointed him. Occasionally she would come and get him for a family reunion whenever her mother was in town I guess to impress her mother. Oh by the way, I have to mention her mother didn't have time for her either so I guess it's a cycle but at least she gave her daughter to a biological family member and she knew her roots. It was by her own admission after it was too late, that her mother did the same thing to her and she hated her mother for what she had done but as I said before, her mom at least kept her in the family. If she had these thoughts about her mom, then why didn't she feel her own son's pain, and try to be a part of whatever he was involved in, he still wanted his mother's support. He loves us I am sure of that and he knows that we love him, but I know without a doubt that he wanted the love of his mother most of all. I "wonder" how a mother can give an innocent baby away without any emotions. It would make sense under certain circumstances, maybe if they were unable to care for them and tried everything possible to keep their child but that was not the case with him. I do not believe that his mother was doing drugs, she had a decent job sometimes two jobs, a place to stay, and a descent car, I guess she had no idea of the damage she was causing. Was the break-up with my son so devastating that she would seek revenge simply because he had moved on with his life and hers was on pause because she was having a baby "maybe she had rejection issues".

I'll admit that we might have spoiled him, showering him with gifts but they were given partly because we wanted him to be happy and "mainly" to soften the pain for him not getting the "ultimate" gift of all times, and that was his "mother's love". He "graduated" from high school at the age of seventeen and she did come to his ceremony so that made him very happy. He was accepted into three colleges and had anticipation of going to one of the three but his mistake was trying to involve his mother. He did not receive any scholarships, I know he would have but his esteem was damaged, and the advance class that he helped some of his classmates with their math and English was not enough. Hoping that she would be as excited about his new adventure in life as he was, he applied for financial aid but needed her signature so that he could get the aid that he needed, she said that she would sign but she did not. He tried asking for her help purchasing his books, even though it was not quite official of course, she agreed to help but that was another lie that she told, she stopped taking his phone calls (another rejection). His plans were to enroll in college at the end of the summer that same year but he did not get the help needed from her. His father or I would have signed if we could have but the paper specifically stated biological parents only we found out after classes had started that we could have. It was too late for him to enroll so he got a job and with the excitement getting his paycheck, he splurged on himself and did not set aside any funds for school. He still had the desire to enroll into college and major in accounting because he loved solving problems, anything dealing with numbers and he wanted to minor in computer science.

A year and half had past and with the help of my daughter he was finally enrolled in school but he was still obsessed with his mother, he called her and ask again if she would help him purchase books and again she said that she would help. We could have gotten them for him but he was seemed to be determined for her to be apart of his life and he told us that she was going to help. He attempted to call her again to remind her of what she had promised him and was antagonized yet again; she stopped answering his phone calls. His anger had finally surfaced he smashed his cell phone against the wall breaking it into many pieces; we realized that he still "had" rejection issues.

I can't go into details at this point because of the case is pending but it is "alleged", that he was involved in a robbery and once again we had to get "psychiatric" help and he was placed on a prescription drug called "Zoloft". He is awaiting trial, instead of working with numbers, he is now a number himself, and that is what has let me inside the jailhouse to know what happens. He's been "poked" in the eye I don't know why, I saw for myself that his eye was a deep purple but he has assured me that he's going to be okay I guess he told me that so that I wouldn't worry. He's along with the rest of the inmates have to do "naked" push-up, "naked" head counts, he washes his clothes by hand if not, his would be thrown in a pile to be washed all together I was told with only water (now the latter came from someone that's never been inside). The incident that occurred with his eye has gotten him L.O.P. (lost of privileges) which means that he and others cannot purchase anything for thirty-five days. If he runs out of toothpaste or soap, then he will just have to do without for the duration. I "wonder" why some of them just do not give a darn when they are released then I wonder why we have had such an increase in crime.

Could it be because they are being bred like "pit bulls or "rooster"'?

He called me and said, Granny half of these kids think that this is joke and most of them cannot read or write very well. Some cannot manage their on money that is on their book so to pass the time and keep his sanity, he is teaching some of them to read and spell, and he is managing several of their funds because some cannot count. His ordeal is the reason that I took this journey; and for those of you that say he is just a jailbird and he will tell me anything, I say to you, I know him, his background, his mannerism, and his capabilities. As I stated throughout this journey I am "not" a writer, this is "reality" speaking because of I am truly disturb at what I have seen through the years. The words, ~Let Freedom Ring" have taken on a "new" meaning and we are all now suffering the consequences. I "wonder" who's really creating the problem, is it the criminal or, those that "expose" a little bit too much of their body, or those that "over price" things that those that are lest fortunate can't afford but try to have. Could it be the movies and television that "glamorizes" sex and extremely violent crimes or the parents that "neglect" or "abandon" their children "hmm" (I wonder).

MY JOURNEY'S END (FOR NOW)

Therefore, everyone will know, this was not to offend anyone in particular but if it did, remember the "rock". I am merely expressing "my" thoughts on "how it was" when we were colored, that's when parents mainly the mother and the "village" in the neighborhood had control of the children, the father was the bread winner and only stepping in to discipline when punishment called for a more demanding approach.

I see "how it is" now because of inflation, both parents have to work and in many cases there are "one" parent households and it is usually just the mother with many children that have different "irresponsible" daddies. Kids are now being "pacified" with video games (some extremely violent). They now can watch television shows that contain explicit "sex" scenes, TV Series that takes them inside the prison walls but "not" showing the filthy conditions that they are confined to as I mentioned earlier. They are impressed by "celebrities" that's became "famous" after selling drugs, gang banging being shot several times, or they were "pimps" that still support the "annual" pimp conventions and now they are all millionaires. I "wonder" why no one observes that kids see the prison system as a "gateway" to success. This is a "repeat" but I can't express it enough it is also "reality writing", remember?

I can imagine "how it will be" in the future, prisons being "incubators" breeding violent criminals because they are exposed to everything and its mostly negative while incarcerated, or S.C.U. could be an "educator" teaching them how to be positive "productive" citizens when their time is up. For those of you that ask the question, "why should they get special treatments?" My answer to you is as I stated earlier, some have low or no self-esteem, abusive parents (mental or physical) or parents that just gave them away as if they were "used clothes". (Some of you knows what I'm talking about) and some just didn't have a chance from day one because of illiterate parents so my question to you is, "which would you rather" someone that comes out "educated" or someone that comes out "extremely" dangerous (hmmm)?

I am at the end of my journey for right now and I sure hope that someone has visualized what I "think" and try to intercede to make a "difference".

As I stated before that this journey was not to "offend" anyone but merely to open eyes to see the things that I "wonder".

I extend this olive branch just in case.

THE INTERCESSOR

(By Norris Williams II)
ROM 8:1-37

Blessed is the person
Who stands in the gap for others
To serve as a bridge
To help your sisters and brothers
In a world with lots of problems
Filled with people with many needs
When Satan toys at their mind
You have to intercede

To be an intercessor
You have to have the faith
To pray for things not seen
And then to eagerly wait
You must pray in the spirit
For those who've made confessions
With groaning that can't uttered
The spirit makes intercession

Many times, there are those you pray for
Are often not aware
They're receiving a special blessing
A result from intercessory prayer
So keep bridging the gap for others
As Jesus bridged the gap for our sins
You are standing in good company
For this, I know we'll win

So when Satan tries to take over
As he often is the aggressor
He always seems to underestimate
The Power of the Intercessor

THE ART GALLERY

The young students attending S.C.U.

The Billion-Dollar Empire

Drawn by an eighteen-year-old Inmate in the county jail

Hand made from "Scratch"

A pop-up mothers day card hand made by a young "inmate"

Dria

This picture was drawn from a snapshot by a student attending S.C.U.

Geroy

This is a hand painting compliments from another student
attending S.C.U.

NOTE

When I started this journey, my grandson's case was pending. Since then he has been sentence to two twenty-five year sentences running concurrent. His lawyer received approximately sixteen thousand dollars to defend him but it never went to trial (he did not do very much). He was frightened into signing a plea bargain even though he had reputable people to vouch for his true character and they knew his tribulations. Even after the conviction, his lawyer expected more money. That would have been all right had I gotten something for the money that I had paid him. I am not saying he (my grandson) should have been release, but allow the teachers lawyer, counselors and psychiatrist that knew him speak. (That never happened) now I "wonder" if I am still here and he survives, what personality will return, home, a" degreed" criminologist or a humble and manner able person.

I also wonder, what career choice the other inmates will choose when they graduate? Alternatively will it be the gifts given to them by "The Creator" or a degree from S.C.U. in P.H.S.O.

[Most of them will not get job offers]

THANK YOU

Thanks to my Sister, Mary Carrier her children, Herman Damon, Chavauna Karen and my niece June Adams for all of your support, thanks.

To a very good friend Patricia Marshall, for cheering me on and allowing me to call on her any time.

To Tasha Jack for staying by my side in my time of sorrow and for being a very good friend to Nicole regardless of what the mood was. Thanks

Thank you so much Anthony Kay owner of Pruitt's Mortuary you are truly the best. You are patient, compassionate, and understanding I will never forget your kindness.

To Alice McKinney I thank you for being a good teacher and a second mother to Nicole.

Drexel Stewart you always stand in the gap when called on and I thank you so much for being a real friend to my family.

To Jackie Lall for being a good friend and listener

Chauncy Williams (my son) for your financial support, thank you.

To Norris Williams II (my son) for allowing me to use poetry from his book titled "Beyond the Zone" thank you.

Clip art; provided by Microsoft word.

ABOUT THE AUTHOR

The reason for this journey is to let readers see her thoughts about things from all aspect. To make people (those interested) know, everything is "not" just black and white [there is always a gray area] but overlooked. This book is a combination of her thoughts that will let you view things from another angle but keep in mind, these are just her thoughts and you are just on her journey. She is not a writer, just a thinker so what you read is "reality" writing, not professional. Punctuations, syllables, and sentence structure maybe wrong but you will get the message "She hopes".

    She is a deep thinker sharing her thoughts and likes to evaluate a situation before passing judgment. She likes to motivate when she recognize gifts in people and tries to encourage them to follow that gift. She has sympathy for those with very low self-esteem and will stay with them to try helping them realize that there is a bright side. She looks for the good in a person when others only focus on the bad because there is good and bad in us all. She is a high school graduate with two years of college with out a degree, mother of three and has retired from her job after thirty years. She watches a lot of news and that keeps her wondering, is it news or just gossip. She is not a Politian and she is not a professor, she just sits in her room, watch T.V. and analyze what she see and hear "They do not always speak for her".